Scarf Neck Cardigan
Crochet Pattern

A crochet motif pattern for a lace-back cardigan sweater with scarf-like front drape.

By Kristen Stein

© 2021 by Kristen Stein. StudioArtworks.com.

All rights reserved. This book or any portion thereof may not be reproduced or used in any manner whatsoever without the expressed written consent of the author.

ISBN: 9798703015315

Contents

Motif Lace Crochet
Pattern Notes
    Figure 1: Order of Motifs and Side Joins
    Notes on the "Joining Round"
Stitches Used & Abbreviations
Pattern
    Yarn
    Hook
    Gauge
    Finished Size
The Motif Pattern
    Motifs 2-25
    Special Motifs: Motifs 19-22
Cardigan Ribbed Trim
    Front and Neckline Ribbing
    Bottom Edge Ribbing
Sleeves
    Sleeve Ribbing
    Wrist Motifs
Finishing Touches & Blocking
Concluding Remarks
Other Recent Pattern Books
Stitch Glossary
About the Artist & Designer

Scarf Neck Cardigan Crochet Pattern

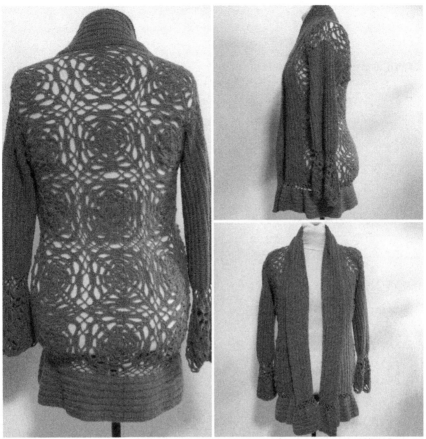

Photo 1: Completed Garment. Shown on Large Mannequin with hip circumference = 42"(105cm)

Motif Lace Crochet

Introduction
I love crocheting garments using lace-inspired motifs. They are a quick and relatively easy way to create crocheted fabric that can be made into beautiful, lacy, and flexible garments or accessories. Motif crochet uses repeated patterns to create individual motifs that are joined together to create an overall crocheted fabric. The designer then creates a garment using the crocheted fabric in much the same way that one would sew a

pattern using regular yards of fabric.

Photo 2: A few of my other patterns using Motif Lace Crochet.

What makes motif crochet fun and flexible is that it is usually accomplished with relatively simple repeated rounds. This breaks up the monotony of row by row stitches and allows the designer greater control over the shape of the final crocheted fabric or garment. By joining the motifs to one another during the final round, the designer is able to create a seamless crocheted fabric that is loose, flexible and drapes beautifully across the body.

Scarf Neck Cardigan Crochet Pattern

Photo 3: Example of Motif Crochet Panel

The fabric created with motifs usually has significant stretch given the lacy open areas created by the joining stitches. This additional stretch is great because it allows the garment to adapt well to many different body shapes and sizes. The overall size of the garment will be determined after stretching and blocking the garment at the end of the creation process. By properly blocking the garment at the end of the crocheting process, you'll be able to create a garment with the ideal dimensions for your body size and shape.

Motif crocheted fabric can also be modified easily in the sense that you can increase or decrease sizes by simply changing the hook size, or modifying the number of rounds of each motif. This way, you can easily turn a top into a tunic, a scarf into a wrap, or a short-sleeve to a long-sleeve by simply adding additional motifs.

The fabric crocheted with motifs is also forgiving. It is difficult to see errors made in the stitches because the design is flexible, open and the stitches move in many directions. Unlike repeated rows, it is visually more difficult to see a skipped or dropped stitch. This is extremely useful as you begin to make your garment because you don't have to be bothered by small mistakes that you might have made. They are often absorbed into the lacework and visually missed by anyone viewing the completed project.

Another wonderful feature of a lace motif garment is that there are rarely any shoulder or side seams. In most cases, the garment is created by joining motifs during their final rounds. This makes it convenient if you accidentally wear the garment 'inside out' as there are no seams to see. But, a possible drawback from this approach is that there are two yarn tails to each motif that must be woven in as you go, or woven in at the end of each motif connection. You will want to leave the ends long enough to weave them into the garment. That way, you won't have a bunch of yarn ends poking out of the final garment. I try to incorporate the yarn ends into each new motif as I go. That way, I don't have to hunt for all of them at the end of the final project.

The beauty of the crocheted motif fabric is not only in the design of the motif itself, but also in the way in which the motifs join together. The design created from the joining stitches can sometimes be just as intricate as the details within the actual motif. You'll notice this when you block the garment and actually get to wear the finished piece. The contrast between the light and dark areas created by the stitches makes for a visually appealing garment that looks beautiful from all angles.

In this pattern, the motifs are not difficult to crochet. They use very straightforward stitches. The end result, however, looks like an intricate series of stitches yielding a romantic lace-inspired cardigan. Although, it may look complicated to make, it truly is not difficult to replicate. The motifs are actually quite simple once you start creating them. The intricate stitch work and lace-inspired look comes from how the motifs are designed and connected to one another during each final round of the motif pattern.

Scarf Neck Cardigan Crochet Pattern

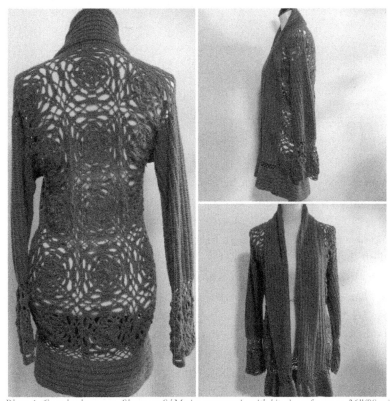

Photo 4: Completed garment. Shown on S/M size mannequin with hip circumference = 36"(90cm)

Pattern Notes

When creating my garment designs, I usually create my own patterned paper and then draw out my designs connecting shapes as I go. I decide what geometric shapes work best for the garment that I am making. I found that certain shapes fit better together and provide a visually appealing final product. Given how many lines and grids I was drawing by hand, I decided to create patterned paper to aid in my design process. I recently added a few of these design notebooks to my Amazon Author page. These books are filled with lined pages and patterned pages of (squares, hexagons and other geometric shapes.) These patterned notebooks should prove useful to fashion designers especially those that knit, crochet, sew or quilt. A few of the design books are shown in the next image. Additional information about these sketch & design books are available in the back of the book.

Additional sketch and design books are also available. Visit my Amazon author page or blog for more information.

Photo 5: New line of designer's notebooks and sketchbooks to aid in the design process.

The pattern for my "Scarf Neck Cardigan" consists of 31 motifs: 25 for the cardigan back & sides; 6 for the lace trim on the sleeves. The garment is written as a "one-size-fits" most pattern, but I provide suggestions on increasing the overall size for a more drapey loose fit if desired.

The motifs will be connected to one another in a certain order as you crochet thereby creating a beautiful seamless garment. (See Figure 1.) We will use 'joining stitches' as we progress through the pattern to join motifs to previously-created motifs and build our "crocheted fabric". This will be explained in more detail when we get to the section called "The Joining Round".

The motif pattern for the capelet consists of square motifs that measure approximately 5.5"(14cm) wide along one edge

Due to its design, the motif will have significant ability to stretch. We will stretch the item to fit (if needed) when we get to the blocking stage at the end of the pattern. The extra stretch of the motif will provide incredible comfort and a great fit for a variety of body shapes and sizes.

Photo 6: One Complete Motif

Figure 1: Order of Motifs and Side Joins

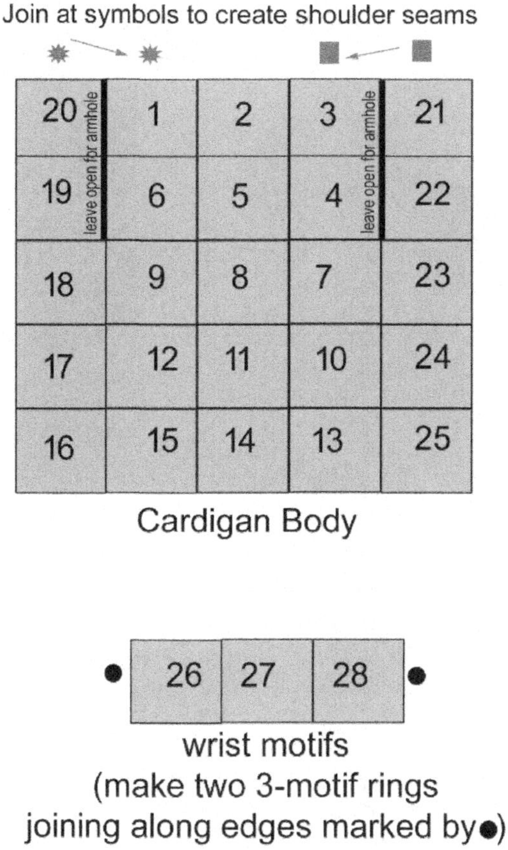

Join at symbols to create shoulder seams

20 (leave open for armhole)	1	2	3 (leave open for armhole)	21
19	6	5	4	22
18	9	8	7	23
17	12	11	10	24
16	15	14	13	25

Cardigan Body

| • | 26 | 27 | 28 | • |

wrist motifs
(make two 3-motif rings
joining along edges marked by •)

Figure 1: Order of Motifs and Side Joins

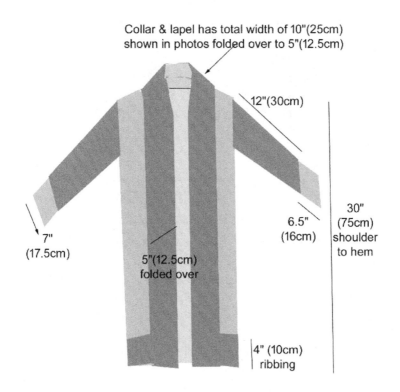

Figure 2: Approximate Garment Dimensions (laid flat after blocking)

Notes on the "Joining Round"

The lace portion of the cardigan body is created "seamlessly as-you-go" in the sense that each motif is joined to an existing motif as you crochet. You will start with Motif 1 and continue to Motif 25 joining motifs according to Figure 1. Each motif is crocheted in 13 rounds. The first 12 rounds are the "preliminary rounds". Round 13 is the "final round". Each motif is "joined" to previous motifs during the motif's final round. The final round is also called the "joining round". In this pattern, Motif 1 will be made from start to finish with a final round that does not join to another motif.

Referring back to Figure 1, Motif 1 is our starting motif. Each additional motif will be made with the preliminary rounds and then 'joined' to existing motifs during its final "joining" round. The joins are created with chain stitches. You will accomplish the 'join' by breaking up the designated chain stitch halfway through its creation. For instance, in this pattern, the joining chain spaces are created as chain 4 loop in the corners, and chain 6 loops along the sides. We create the "join" during the final round by creating half the number of chain stitches and then joining with a slip stitch to the corresponding corner or side on a previously-made motif. We then complete the chain 4 or the chain 6 to 'complete the chain' and continue to work the final round on the motif we are making. This joining process will feel like a 'zig-zag' movement between the motif "in progress" and previously completed motifs that you are seamlessly joining into the crocheted garment. We join as we go in order to allow the garment and crocheted fabric to take shape. For this garment, we will join motifs to one another in the order illustrated by Figure 1. (**Designer note**: When you begin making the garment, you might want to print out a copy of Figure 1 so that you can use it for quick reference.)

Here are a few additional notes to further illustrate the joining process. This will be discussed in more detail when we get to the actual pattern.

Looking back at Figure 1, you see that Motif 1 is crocheted as one complete motif using the pattern Rounds 1-13. When you complete Round 13, you'll fasten off and weave in the yarn ends. Then, you will start Motif 2 and complete Rounds 1-12. Then, you'll start the final Round 13 that will consist of one side that will be joined along two consecutive corners to the existing Motif 1. Once the shared edge is 'joined', you'll continue to finish the remaining sides of Motif 2 without joining them to another motif. You'll fasten off Motif 2, weave in ends and then move onto Motif 3. We will discuss each of the Motif joins in greater detail when we move onto the actual pattern.

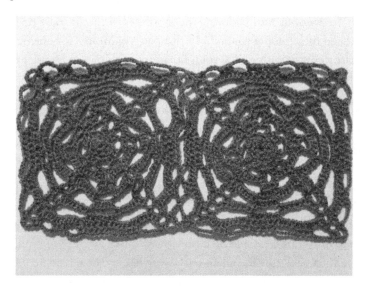

Photo 7: The first 2 joined Motifs with one shared edge.

Special "Joining Rounds"

There are a few motifs that have "special joining rounds". These are identified with bold shapes & symbols in Figure 1. These special shapes & symbols identify the motifs whose edges join together to seamlessly connect the front and the back of the garment. For the shoulder seams and arm openings, the special joining edges will occur when we get to Motifs 19-22. These "special joining rounds" that seamlessly connect front and back will be discussed in more detail within the pattern. (There will be special joining rounds for the wrist rings too if you decide to add the lace trim wrist sections.)

Once you successfully join Motifs 1-25, the motif portion of the cardigan body is complete. You will then add wide ribbing to the neckline, bottom perimeter and sleeves. You will then have the option of adding lace motifs to the wrist area of the sleeve. If you add this additional lace portion, you'll make two 3-motif rings using the same square motif pattern you used for the cardigan body. Lastly, you will block the garment to your desired dimensions or use the dimensions that I provide in the pattern.

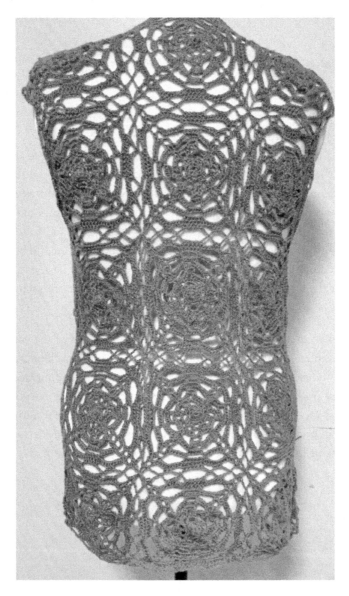

Photo 8: Motif portion of cardigan body.

Scarf Neck Cardigan Crochet Pattern

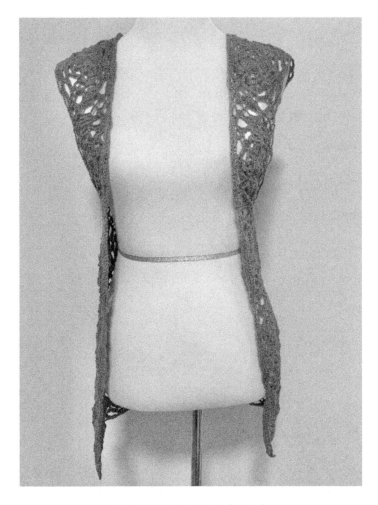

Photo 9: Motif portion of cardigan body.

Stitches Used & Abbreviations

(A **stitch glossary** is provided at the end of the pattern.)

Chain (ch)

Back-Loop-Only (BLO)

Double-Crochet (dc)

Half-Double-Crochet (hdc)

Single-Crochet (sc)

Slip Stitch (sl st)

Other Abbreviations you might see in this pattern:

Pattern (Pat)

Repeat (Rep)

Right-Side (RS)

Round (Rd)

Skip (sk)

Space (sp)

Wrong Side (WS)

Yarn Over (YO)

Pattern

Materials used:

Yarn
About 3100 yds. Super-fine (#1).

As shown: 5 skeins of Loops & Threads Woolike Simili-Laine in Sage. Each skein is 678 yards (620m) / 3.5 oz (100g).

Hook
Crochet Hook 3.5mm or size needed to obtain gauge.

Gauge
24dc stitches and 12 rows = 4" (10cm)

The motif should measure approximately 2.5" (6.25cm) along one motif edge after Round 7 and 5"(12.5cm) after Round 12.

The completed motif, after Round 13, should measure approximately 5.5"(14.5cm) across one motif edge.

Finished Size
Sizes:
The cardigan is written as a 'one-size-fits most' pattern. It is open styling with significant drape in front and fitted across the back to show off the lacy details. The back shoulder-to-shoulder measures approximately 16"(42cm)-18"(45cm) unstretched. To increase the overall size of the cardigan and add extra drape to the back, you can add an extra column of

motifs in the center back or use a larger crochet hook and/or thicker dk-weight yarn to create larger motifs.

From shoulder to base, the cardigan measures 30"(75cm) in length. The total perimeter width is about 52"(130cm) with about 20"-24"(50cm-60cm) across the back from side-to-side with the extra drape in front. The scarf-like neckline is a total of 10"(25cm) wide and folds over to about 5"(12.5cm) wide. The ribbed portion of sleeve is 12"(30cm) long with an extra 6.5"(16cm) of lace trim around wrist.

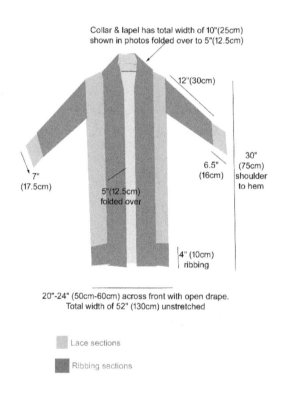

Photo 10: Approximate Garment Measurements (laid flat). Unstretched after blocking.

Scarf Neck Cardigan Crochet Pattern

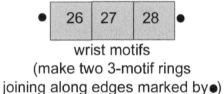

Figure 1: Order of Motifs and Side Joins

Figure 1 is repeated here for easy viewing while reading the pattern. When you begin making the garment, you might want to print out a copy of Figure 1 so that you can use it for quick reference.

Photo 11: The completed Motif.

The Motif Pattern

(Refer back to Figure 1 to join the motifs as you go. You'll need to connect the motifs on certain sides as you complete the final round of each motif. See my pattern notes at the beginning of this book for a better understanding of how to join the motifs as you proceed. The joining process will also be discussed in more detail as we progress through the pattern.)

Round 1 (Rd1): Ch4. Slip stitch in starting chain stitch to form a ring.

Rd 2: ch3(acts as 1st dc); 7 dc in ring. Slip stitch in top of starting ch-3 to end the round.

End with 8 dc stitches.

Rd 3: sc in starting stitch; *ch4; skip 1 dc; sc in next dc**; repeat from * to ** around. Slip stitch in opening sc to end the round.

End with 4 ch-4 spaces.

Rd4: (2hdc, ch6, 2hdc) in each ch-4 space around. Slip stitch in first hdc to end the round.

End with 4 ch-6 spaces.

Photo 12: The motif after Round 4.

Rd 5:. Sc in opening stitch; ch3; *(2hdc, ch6, 2hdc) in next ch-6 space; ch3; skip 1hdc***; sc in next hdc; ch3**; repeat from * to ** around. On final repeat, end at *** and slip stitch in starting sc to end the round.

End with 8 ch-3 spaces and 4 ch-6 spaces.

Photo 13: The motif after Round 5.

Rd6: 4hdc in first ch-3 space; *(2hdc, ch6, 2hdc) in next ch-6 space; 4hdc in next ch-3 space***; 4hdc in next ch-3 space**; repeat from * to ** around. On final repeat end at *** and slip stitch in first hdc to end the round.

End with 4 ch-6 spaces.

Photo 14: The motif after Round 6.

Rd 7: sc in starting stitch; ch6; sc in same starting stitch to create a loop; *ch5; skip 6 hdc; 6hdc in next ch-6 space; ch5; skip 6 hdc***; (sc, ch6, sc) in next hdc**; repeat from * to ** around. On final repeat, end at *** and slip stitch to starting sc to end the round.

End with 4 ch-6 spaces and 8 ch-5 spaces. Check your gauge. Your motif should measure approximately 2.5"(6.25cm) wide along one edge.

Photo 15: Motif after Round 7.

Rd 8: Slip stitch into 1st ch-6 space; [ch2 (acts as 1st hdc), hdc, ch6, 2hdc] in same ch-6 space; *6hdc in next ch-5 space; ch5; 6hdc in next ch-5 space***; (2hdc, ch6, 2hdc) in next ch-6 space**; repeat from * to ** around. On final repeat, end at *** and slip stitch in top of starting ch-2 to end the round.

End with 4 ch-5 spaces and 4 ch-6 spaces.

Photo 16: Motif after Round 8.

Rd 9: Slip stitch in 1st ch-6 space; [ch2(acts as 1st hdc), hdc, ch6, 2hdc] in same ch-6 space; *ch6; 6hdc in next ch-5 space; ch6***; (2hdc, ch6, 2hdc) in next ch-6 space**; repeat from * to ** around. On final repeat, end at *** and slip stitch in top of starting ch-2 to end the round.

End with 8 ch-6 "side" spaces and 4 ch-6 "corner spaces".

Photo 17: Motif after Round 9.

Note: Beginning with Round 10, the corner spaces will now have a ch-4 loop rather than a ch-6 loop.

Rd 10: Slip stitch in 1st ch-6 space; [ch2(acts as 1st hdc), hdc, **ch4**, 2hdc] in same ch-6 space; *6hdc in next ch-6 space; ch6; 6hdc in next ch-6 space***; (2hdc, **ch4**, 2hdc) in next ch-6 space**; repeat from * to ** around. On final repeat, end at *** and slip stitch in top of starting ch-2 to end the round.

End with 4 ch-6 side spaces and 4 ch-4 corner spaces.

Scarf Neck Cardigan Crochet Pattern

Photo 18: Motif after Round 10.

Rd 11: Slip stitch in 1st ch-4 corner space; (ch2, hdc, ch4, 2hdc) in same ch-4 corner space; ***ch9**; 6hdc in next ch-6 space; **ch9*****; (2hdc, **ch4**, 2hdc) in next ch-4 corner space**; repeat from * to ** around. On final repeat, end at *** and slip stitch in top of starting ch-2 to end the round.

End with 8 ch-9 side spaces and 4 ch-4 corner spaces.

Rd 12: Slip stitch in 1st ch-4 corner space; (ch2, hdc, ch4, 2hdc) in same ch-4 corner space; *9hdc in next ch-9 space; hdc in each of next 6 hdc stitches; 9hdc in next ch-9 space***; (2hdc, ch4, 2hdc) in next ch-4 corner space**; repeat from * to ** around. On final repeat, end at *** and slip stitch in top of starting ch-2 to end the round.

End with 24 hdc along edge and (2hdc, ch4, 2hdc) pattern in each corner.

Rd 13: (Final "Joining" Rd) Remember: For Motif 1 we will do the complete Round 13 without joining to other motifs. For all other motifs at least one side will be a joining edge to join with one or more other motifs that you have already made. Refer to Figure 1 and the Pattern Notes at the beginning of the book to review the joining rounds and the special joins. It is easiest to start joining in the first **ch4** corner space between clusters. The joining process for all Motifs other than Motif 1 are indicated by the bold typeface below.

Slip stitch in 1st ch-4 space; (ch2, hdc, **ch4**, 2hdc) in same ch-4 corner space; ***ch6**; skip 2 hdc stitches of corner pattern; skip 3 hdc stitches along side edge; hdc in each of next 3 hdc stitches; **ch6**; skip 3 hdc stitches; hdc in each of next 6 hdc stitches in center side edge; **ch6**; skip 3 hdc stitches; hdc in each of next 3 hdc stitches; **ch6**; skip 3 hdc stitches at end of side edge***; skip 2 hdc stitches of next corner pattern; (2hdc, **ch4**, 2hdc) in next ch-4 corner space**. Repeat from * to ** around. On final repeat, end at *** and slip stitch in top of starting ch2 to end the round.

Fasten off. Weave in ends.

End with 4 ch-6 side spaces (16 spaces in total) and 4 ch-4 corner spaces that will be used for joining motifs as we build the garment.

After the final Round 13, one edge of the Motif should measure about 5.5" (14.5cm) wide from one ch-4 corner to the next ch-4. (unstretched)

(**Note:** The stitches highlighted in bold identify the stitches that are the joining stitches. In all motifs (other than Motif 1), you will substitute (**ch2, slip stitch to other motif, ch2**) in place of the **ch4** on all loops requiring a ch4 join. You'll substitute (**ch3, slip stitch to other motif, ch3**) in place of the **ch6** on all loops requiring a ch6 join. If you are not joining a side or corner, then do the final round using a ch4 or ch6 without a joining stitch in the middle. Continue to create the final round joining in the spaces as needed to create the garment according to Figure 1.)

Photo 19: Motif 1 after the Final Round.

Congratulations! Motif 1 is a now complete. The motif should measure approximately 5.5" (14.5cm) unstretched along one side edge.

Motifs 2-25

Now we will begin to make the other motifs that make up the cardigan body. Motifs 2-15 will make up the cardigan back. Motifs 16-25 will make up the lace side edges. Motifs 2-25 will begin just like Motif 1. You'll make them the same way through the preliminary rounds 1-12. It's only the final "joining" round (Round 13) that differs. During the "join" you won't create a ch4 or a ch6 in the joining positions. You will instead break these chains in half and slip stitch to the corresponding space on a previously made motif to seamlessly join them together. You'll then complete the ch4 or the ch6 when you return back to the final round of the motif on which you are working. In this way, you will mimic the ch4 or the ch6 spaces, but you are able to seamlessly pick up other motifs as you go. This should feel like a 'zig-zag' movement between the current motif on which you are working and the previously made motifs that you are joining.

For example, here is how you will create Motif 2 and join it to the previously made Motif 1.

Repeat **Rd1-Rd12** of the Motif Pattern in the same way you made Motif 1.

When you get to the final round, do the following:

Motif 2's Joining Round (Rd13):

We will begin the join in the first corner of Motif 2 and zig-zag between Motif 2 and Motif 1 to pick up Motif 1 using the ch4 and ch6 loops.

Let's begin:

Slip stitch in 1st ch-4 space of Motif 2; (ch2, hdc, **ch2, slip stitch in first ch-4 corner space between clusters on Motif 1, ch2**, 2hdc) in ch-4 starting ch-4 corner space on Motif 2; **ch3, slip stitch in next ch-6 space on Motif 1, ch3**; skip 2 hdc stitches of corner pattern of Motif 2; skip 3 hdc stitches along side edge of Motif 2; hdc in each of next 3 hdc stitches on Motif 2; **ch3, slip stitch in next ch-6 space on Motif 1, ch3**; skip 3 hdc stitches on Motif 2; hdc in each of next 6 hdc stitches in center side edge of Motif 2; **ch3, slip stitch in next ch-6 space on Motif 1, ch3**; skip 3 hdc stitches on Motif 2; hdc in each of next 3 hdc stitches on Motif 2; **ch3, slip stitch in next ch-6 space on Motif 1, ch3**; skip 3 hdc stitches at end of side edge of Motif 2; skip 2 hdc stitches of next corner pattern on Motif 2; (2hdc, **ch2, slip stitch in next ch-4 corner space between clusters on Motif 1, ch2**, 2hdc) in next ch-4 corner space of Motif 2.

You have now joined one complete side of Motif 2 to Motif 1 using two consecutive ch-4 corners. Work the remaining edges of Motif 2 just like the final round of Motif 1 without using any joining slip stitches to other motifs. The remaining edges will be completed with regular ch-4 and ch-6 spaces without the additional joining slip stitch. Fasten off when you get to the end and weave in the ends. Move onto Motif 3.

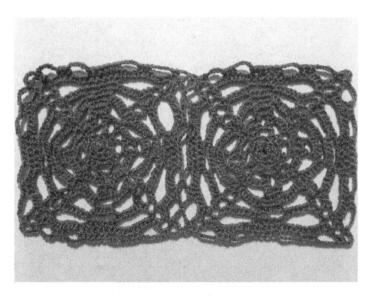

Photo 20: Motif 2 joined to Motif 1 along shared edge.

Motif 3: Looking back at Figure 1, you can see that Motif 3 joins on only one of its four edges. Motif 3 will join to previously made Motif 2 along Motif 2's side edge. All other edges are completed as unjoined edges just like how you created Motif 1.

Motif 4 joins to Motif 3 along Motif 4's top edge. All other edges are completed as unjoined edges during the Final Round.

Motif 5 is the first motif that joins on more than one edge. Looking at Figure 1, you can see that Motif 5 joins to both Motif 4 and Motif 2. Start by joining Motif 5 to Motif 4 along Motif 4's side edge and then join to Motif 2 along Motif 2's bottom edge. The remaining two edges are completed as unjoined edges.

Motif 6-15: Continue to join motifs according to Figure 1 to complete the cardigan back panel (Motifs 1-15)

Photo 21: Motifs 1-12.

Motifs 16-18: Create and join Motifs 16-18 of the side edge in the same way that you created Motifs 1-15 of the back panel.

Special Motifs: Motifs 19-22

Looking back at Figure 1, you'll see that **Motif 19** is first Motif that is considered a special join. Notice that Motif 19 creates our first arm opening. We will join Motif 19 to Motif 18 along only one edge. The remaining edges are completed as unjoined edges as we complete Motif 19's final round.

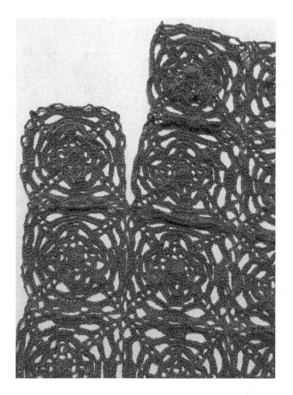

Photo 22: Garment after adding Motif 19 (beginning of arm opening created)

Motif 20: Motif 20 is another special join. This motif will complete the arm opening and also fold over and join to Motif 1 to create the seamless shoulder join.

It is easiest to join consecutive edges working from the rightmost corner and continue in a counter-clockwise direction. Begin by joining Motif 20 to Motif 19 along Motif 19's top edge; work the next edge of Motif 20 as an unjoined edge in order to complete the armhole opening. Join the 3rd edge of Motif 20 to the top edge of Motif 1 to create the seamless shoulder join. Then create the 4th edge of Motif 20 as an unjoined edge.

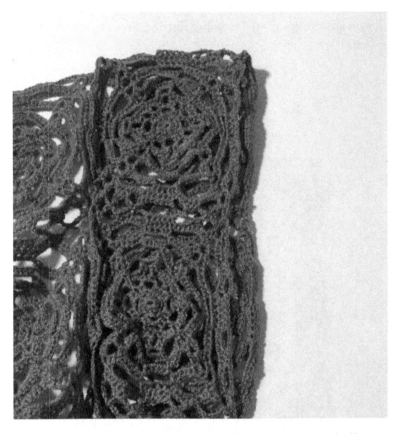

Photo 23: Motif 20 on the top after joining to Motifs 19 and Motif 1 (to create shoulder join)

Motif 21: Motif 21 is another of the special joins. Motif 21 creates the shoulder join on the opposite side of the cardigan panel. Motif 21 joins to only Motif 3 along Motif 3's top edge. All three remaining edges of Motif 21 are completed as unjoined edges when working the final round of the pattern.

Motif 22: Motif 22 is the last of our special joins on the cardigan body. Motif 22 joins to Motif 21 along Motif 21's bottom edge. All other edges are completed as unjoined edges.

Complete **Motifs 23-25** in the same way that you did Motifs 16-18 on the opposite side of cardigan body.

Once you successfully join Motif 25, the motif portion of the cardigan body is complete. Eventually, we will be adding 6 more motifs (two 3-motif rings) when we create the decorative lace trim near the wrist of the sleeve. But, I'll explain this motif detail later in the pattern. We will now move onto creating the wide ribbed scarf front and the ribbing along the bottom perimeter.

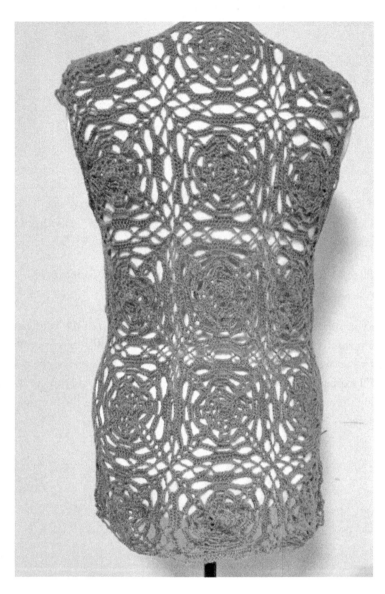

Photo 24: Motif portion of cardigan back.

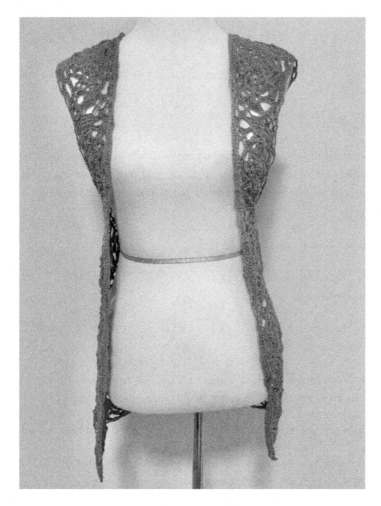

Photo 25: Lace sides (shown on small/med dress form.)

Cardigan Ribbed Trim
Front and Neckline Ribbing

Join yarn in the ch-4 corner space of Motif 25 at the bottom of cardigan front. Moving along front of cardigan, we will make evenly-spaced ch-6 loops around the entire front & neckline.

Let's begin!

Front & Neckline Row 1: sc in starting ch-4 corner space of Motif 25;

*[ch6; sc in next ch-6 space]**4 times**; ch6; sc in last ch-4 corner space of same motif; ch6; sc in ch-4 corner space of next motif**; repeat from * to ** around entire front and neckline until you reach the end of Motif 16. Turn.

End with 65 ch-6 loops made.

Front & Neckline Row 2: Work 6sc in each ch-6 space across front and neckline. Turn.

Front & Neckline Row 3: ch3(acts as 1st dc); dc in each sc around front and neckline.

Front & Neckline Row 4: ch3(acts as 1st dc); dc in back-loop-only (BLO) of every dc thereafter around entire neckline and front edge. Turn.

Front & Neckline Rows 5-12: Repeat Row 4 until you reach Row 12.

(Note: We will now make a few rows of "mesh lace" using ch-6 loops before continuing with more ribbing rows.)

Front & Neckline Row 13: sc in starting stitch; *ch6; skip 5 dc stitches; sc in next dc**; repeat from * to ** across row. End with a ch-6 and sc in last dc to end the row. Turn.

Scarf Neck Cardigan Crochet Pattern

Photo 26: Front and Neckline ribbing up to Row 13.

Photo 27: Front and Neckline Ribbing up to Row 13.

Front & Neckline Row 14: sc in starting stitch; ch6: sc in 1st ch-6 space; *ch6; sc in next ch-6 space**; repeat from * to ** to end of row. On final repeat, instead of a ch-6, create a ch3 and dc in the sc stitch at the end of the row. The combination of a ch3+dc will mimic the length of a ch-6 loop, but will allow us to end in the center of the last ch-6 space which is a better starting position for the next row.

(Note: You should end with one more ch-6 space then you had in Row 13.)

Front & Neckline Row 15: sc in starting space; *ch6; sc in next ch-6 space**; repeat from * to ** to end of row. End with a sc in last ch-6 space. (You should now have the same number of ch-6 spaces that you had in Row 13.) Turn.

Front & Neckline Row 16: Work 6sc in each ch-6 space across. Turn.

Front & Neckline Row 17: ch3(acts as 1st dc); dc in each sc thereafter across row. Turn.

Front & Neckline Rows 18-22: Repeat Row 4 until you get to row 22.

Front & Neckline Rows 23-27: Repeat Rows 13-17.

Front & Neckline Rows 28-38: Repeat Row 4 until you get to Row 38. Do not fasten off. Proceed with Bottom Edge Ribbing in the next section.

Photo 28: Front and neckline ribbing. Complete.

Photo 29: Front and Neckline Ribbing (folded over)

Bottom Edge Ribbing

We will be creating the bottom edge ribbing similar to how we just completed the front and neckline ribbing. First, we will create a row of ch-6 loops across the bottom. You'll notice that the first row is broken up into three parts (A, B and C) to help explain how to equally distribute the ch-6 spaces across the ribbed sections and the motif sections of the bottom edge

Let's begin!

Bottom Edging Row 1:

Row 1: Part A:: sc in 1st stitch of bottom edge. (Where the bottom edge meets the completed front edge.) *[ch6; skip 5 stitches along ribbing rows; sc in next stitch] **6 times across the 12 rows of front panel ribbing****(Note: You'll be single-crocheting in the last stitch of every other row of ribbing); ch6; skip the ch-6 mesh spaces; sc in 1st stitch of next section of ribbing; [ch6; skip 5 stitchers along ribbing rows; sc in next stitch of ribbing]**3 times** across the next 6 rows of ribbing; ch6; skip mesh spaces; sc in 1st stitch of next ribbing section; repeat * to ** one time across the last 12 ribbing rows of the front panel***

Row 1: Part B:: sc in ch-4 corner space of first motif; *[ch6; sc in next ch-6 space]**4 times** across motif edge; ch6; sc in ch-4 corner motif of same motif; ch6; sc in ch-4 corner space of next motif**; repeat from * to ** of "Row 1: Part B" across motif portion of bottom edge.

Row 1: Part C:: sc in 1st stitch of ribbing section; repeat * to *** of "Row 1: Part A"across remaining ribbing rows. End with a sc in final stitch of bottom edge. Turn.

End with 63 ch-6 spaces (or 69 ch-6 spaces if you added an extra column of motifs to back panel.)

Bottom Edging Row 2: sc in starting stitch; ch6; sc in 1st ch-6 space; *ch6; sc in next ch-6 space**; repeat from * to ** across bottom edge. On final repeat instead of a ch-6, create a ch3 and dc in the sc stitch at the end of the row. (The combination of the ch3+dc will mimic the last ch-6 space but the combination allows us to end in the center of the space which is a better starting position for the next row.) Turn.

You should end with one more ch-6 space that you had at the end of Row 1.

Bottom Edging Row 3: sc in your starting ch-6 space; *ch6; sc in next ch-6 space**; repeat from * to ** across row. End with a sc in the last ch-6 space to end the row. You should end with the same number of ch-6 spaces that you had at the end of Row 1. Turn.

Bottom Edging Row 4: Work 6sc in every ch-6 space across row. Turn.

Bottom Edging Row 5: ch3(acts as 1st dc); dc in each sc thereafter across row. Turn.

Bottom Edging Row 6: ch3(acts as 1st dc); dc in BLO in every dc thereafter across row. Turn.

Bottom Edging Rows 7-16: Repeat Row 6 until you reach Row 16 (or your desired length)

Bottom Edging Row 17: sc in each dc across row. Turn.

Bottom Edging Row 18: sc in each sc across row.

Fasten off. Weave in ends. Move onto crocheting the sleeves.

Photo 30: Bottom Edge Ribbing

Sleeves
Sleeve Ribbing
We will now add the sleeves to the cardigan. The sleeves are created with about 12"(30cm) of ribbing from the shoulder to just below the elbow. We will then add lace motif trim to the wrist area of the sleeve that coordinates

with the pattern along the back and sides of the cardigan. If you do not want to add the lace motif wrist section, you can simply create the ribbed sleeve all the way to the wrist. The choice is up to you. I will provide instructions on how to do the ribbing and add the additional motifs. But, you can modify this section to your desired fit.

Let's begin.

Join yarn on the right side of the garment in the ch-4 corner space of one of the motifs in the underarm section.

Armhole Round 1 (Rd1): sc in starting space; *[ch6; sc in next ch-6 space]**4 times** across motif edge; ch6; sc in next ch-4 corner space of same motif; ch6; sc in ch-4 corner space of next motif**; repeat from * to ** across all four motifs of the armhole. Slip stitch to starting sc to end the round.

End with 24 ch-6 loops around armhole.

Armhole Rd2: Work 6sc in each ch-6 space around armhole. Slip stitch in starting sc to end the round.

Do not fasten off. Move onto Sleeve Ribbing.

(Note: We will be adding on about 6"(15cm) of lace to the end of the ribbing. You can add a longer starting chain if you do not want to add the lace to the wrist area.)

Sleeve Ribbing Row 1: Loosely ch73 to create the first row of sleeve ribbing (approximately 12"(30cm)); **dc** in third chain from hook and in each chain stitch thereafter until you reach the armhole edge on the cardigan body; skip 3 sc stitches of armhole edge ; slip stitch in each of next 3 sc stitches of armhole (this is the height needed to create the next row of ribbing). Turn.

End with 70dc of ribbing in first row.

Sleeve Ribbing Row 2: Working back up the Ribbing Row, dc in the BLO of each dc to the end of the sleeve ribbing. Turn.

End with 70dc in ribbing.

Sleeve Ribbing Row 3: ch3(acts as first dc); dc in BLO of every dc thereafter until you return to the armhole edge of the cardigan body; skip 3 sc stitches of armhole edge; slip stitch in each of next 3 sc stitches of armhole edge (to move along the armhole and create the height needed for the next row of ribbing.) Turn.

You should always have the same number of stitches at the end of each row of the ribbing. (In my case 70 stitches.)

Repeat Rows 2 & 3 all the way around armhole.

I ended with 48 rows of ribbing.

Seam the edges together: On your final row, end with a completed Row 2 and then place the right sides together and use a single-crochet stitch along the wrong side of garment to seam the two edges together.

Repeat the Armhole Rounds and Ribbing Rows for second sleeve.

Scarf Neck Cardigan Crochet Pattern

Photo 31: Sleeve Ribbing

Wrist Motifs

We will now crochet two 3-motif rings that we will add to the bottom of the sleeve in the wrist area. The motifs will add about 6"(15cm) to the 12"(30cm) of sleeve ribbing.

Look back at Figure 1 and the Square Motif Pattern to see how to create the 3-motif ring. You will basically create **Motifs 26-28** the same way you created and joined Motifs 1-3 in the cardigan body. Except, you will also want to join one side of Motif 28 to one side of Motif 26 in order to create a ring of three motifs. You will then create and join **Motifs 29-31** to create a ring for the second sleeve. For both of these rings, the first Motif of the ring (i.e. Motif 26 and Motif 29) will be made like Motif 1 as a complete Motif without a joining round. All the remaining motifs will join to existing motifs on at least one side.

You should end with a total of 18 chain spaces (aka "loops") around the perimeter of the motif that we can use to join the lace wrist section to the ribbed sleeve. (You should have 6 ch-4 corner spaces and 12 ch-6 side spaces across the 3-motif ring edge.)

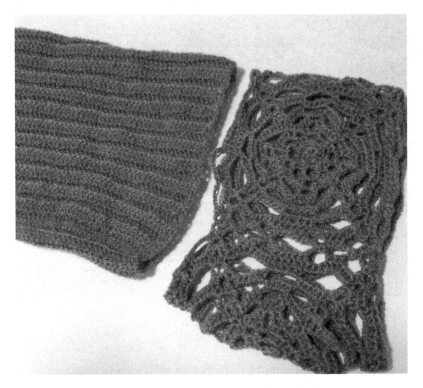

Photo 32: Sleeve Ribbing and Wrist Motif Ring.

Prepare the sleeve for the wrist motif ring.
Before we add the motif ring to the sleeve, we have to create a round of equally-spaced loops on the ribbed sleeve which can be used to join the Motifs to the sleeve.

Wrist Round 1: Join the yarn in one of the stitches in the underside of the sleeve; sc in same starting stitch; **create 18 evenly-spaced ch-6 loops around the ribbed edge of the sleeve.** (Note: For the sleeve pictured above, I created one ch-6 loop every 2.5 ribbed rows. This worked out to one ch-6 space every 8 stitches. It doesn't have to be perfect, just be sure you end with a total of **18 ch-6 loops**. On your final ch-6 space, create a ch3 and dc in the starting sc to end in the center of your last ch-6 space. This will be a better starting position for the next round.

Be sure that you have 18 ch-6 loops.

We will now join the motif ring to the ribbed sleeve in much the same way that we joined motifs together. We will use all 18 spaces around the ribbed sleeve and the motif ring to join the two pieces together. We will use a (ch3, join with motif, ch3) pattern to zig-zag back and forth between the sleeve and the motif ring.

Let's begin!

Wrist Round 2: (Joining Round) sc in starting ch-6 space on sleeve; **(ch3**; slip stitch join to Motif ring using one of the 18 ch-4 or ch-6 spaces around the ring; **ch3);** sc in next ch-6 space on sleeve; ***(ch3;** join in next available ch-4 or ch-6 space on Motif ring; **ch3);** sc in next ch-6 loop on sleeve**; repeat from * to ** around the ring. You should join in all 18 loops. Slip stitch in first sc to end the round.

Fasten off. Weave in ends. Repeat the same Wrist Rounds to finish the second sleeve.

Photo 33: Wrist detail

Congratulations! The cardigan is complete. You will now want to block the garment to your desired specifications, or use my blocking dimensions as your guide. The motifs have a significant ability to stretch, so you will want to shape them to your desired sizes as you block the garment.

Finishing Touches & Blocking

The motif garment that you just completed may require shaping and blocking to achieve the right fit and dimensions. You will want to gently tug on the garment and shape the garment to smooth out the motif edges especially around the joining stitches. You want the edges to seamlessly blend into one another and look like lacework rather than appear as a collection of identifiable shapes. You will notice that the garment gets longer and wider as you gently shape the motifs, especially near the joining stitches. Be careful not to overstretch the garment while smoothing out the corner joins. The design of the garment will stretch as you wear it.

Blocking is very important. This will smooth out the motif joins and the other stitches and give a nice polished look to your joining edges. Block the garment according to your yarn's specification. In most cases, you can simply wet the garment, gently squeeze out the excess moisture and lay it onto a blocking board or towel. Shape the garment into the desired dimensions, or use my dimensions as a guideline. If using a blocking board, pin the edges in place and let dry. Lay flat to dry. Once dry, you can enjoy your new garment!

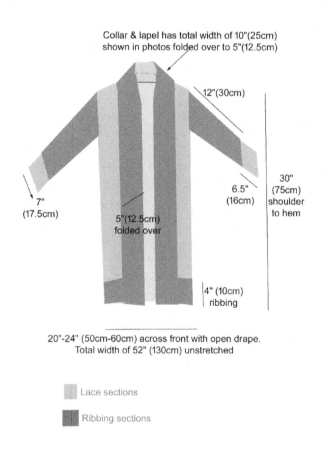

Photo 34: Suggested Dimensions of finished garment when blocking.

Photo 48: Completed garment. Shown on S/M size mannequin with hip circumference = 36"(90cm)

Photo 49: Size 1 side view on Mannequin with Waist 35"(87.5cm)

Photo 50: Completed Garment. Shown on Large Mannequin with hip circumference = 42"(105cm)

Concluding Remarks

Congratulations on completing your "Scarf Neck Cardigan". I hope you enjoyed making this as much as I enjoyed designing it. I hope you agree that lace motif crochet is a beautiful, fast, fun and exciting way to design garments. The pieces are feminine, romantic & delicate. They have a fluidity to them that shape gently across the body and are flattering on all body types. I hope you are pleased with the items that you created and that you enjoyed making the motif garment as much as I enjoyed designing it. If you were pleased with the book, and the pattern in particular, please leave a review. If you discover any errors, or have any questions, please write to me through my amazon author's bookpage, or through my blog at http://kristensteinfineart.blogspot.com. You can also find me on Instagram or TikTok @kristensteindesigns.

I look forward to hearing from you. Please take a look at my other recent pattern books and designing sketchbooks (digital and paperback). I have many other patterns available as shown on the next page.

Other Recent Pattern Books

Most recently added:

Scarf Neck Cardigan Crochet Pattern

Available as eBooks or Paperbacks.

Available as eBooks or Paperbacks Learn more about these titles on my blog: http://kristensteinfineart.blogspot.com
or search Amazon & Ravelry for Kristen Stein.

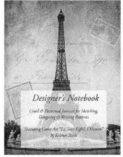

Additional sketch and design books are also available. Visit my Amazon author page or blog for more information.

Photo 35: Designer Sketchbooks.

New line of sketchbook and design books to aid in the design process for fashion designers, especially those that knit, crochet, sew or quilt. The designer's notebooks have both lined and patterned pages to provide an area to sketch out the design and an area to write pattern notes.

Stitch Glossary

Bobble or Cluster – See **"Treble-Crochet-Together Cluster/Bobble"** below.

Chain stitch (ch) - Start with a slipknot. Insert your crochet hook through the slipknot then pick up the yarn with the hook. Pull the yarn through the slip knot back to front. This is the first chain stitch.

Double-crochet (dc) - Yarn over the hook, insert hook into the next stitch to be worked and yarn over again. Pull the yarn through the stitch and yarn over again. You should now have three loops on the hook. Pull the yarn through both loops and yarn over again. Pull yarn through the last two loops on the hook to complete the double crochet.

Double-Crochet Together (specifically dc2tog): Often used to easily decrease stitches by combining two dc stitches into one dc stitch. Yarn over. Insert hook into next stitch. Yarn over. Pull yarn through stitch. You should have three stitches on hook. Yarn over. Pull yarn through first two loops on hook. You should now have two loops on hook. Yarn over. Insert hook in next stitch. Yarn over. Pull yarn through stitch. You should have four loops on hook. Yarn over. Pull through first two loops. Yarn over. Pull yarn through all three loops on hook.

Half-Double-Crochet (hdc) – Similar to a double-crochet, but it ends up with a slightly shorter stitch. Yarn over the hook, insert hook into the next stitch to be worked and yarn over again. Pull the yarn through the stitch and yarn over again. You should now have three loops on the hook. Pull the yarn all three loops to complete the half-double crochet.

Picot (p) – The picot is a decorative stitch that is often used in borders or trim to add a little extra charm or flourish to the final project. The most common picot is the ch3 or ch4 picot. My patterns use the ch3 picot (unless otherwise noted). To create a ch3 picot, simply ch3 and then insert your hook in the third chain from hook. Yarn over and pull through the stitch and through the loop on the hook. Basically, you ch3 and then slip stitch into the first chain of the ch3. This will create a tight little "dot" that adds a nice decorative trim to the final piece.

Single Crochet (sc) - Insert the hook into stitch. Yarnover and pull the yarn through the loop on your hook. Yarn over again and pull the yarn through both loops on your hook. You've created one single crochet stitch.

Slip stitch (sl st) - Slip stitches are convenient for transitioning between rounds and helping to move the yarn or thread to different starting positions without adding height or bulk. To make a slip stitch, insert your hook through the desired space. Hook your yarn and pull it through. You've just made your first slip stitch.

Treble crochet (tr) - Also called a triple crochet. Yarn over your hook twice. Insert the hook into the next stitch. Yarn over and draw the yarn through the stitch. You should have four loops on the hook. Yarn over the hook again and draw the yarn through two of the four loops on the hook. Yarn over again and draw through two more loops. Yarn over again and draw through last two loops. You should be left with one loop on hook to start next stitch.

Treble-Crochet-Together Cluster/Bobble ('trtog cluster/bobble") – This stitch creates a cluster of treble crochets all sharing the same stitch space when complete. *Yarn over twice, insert your hook into stitch, yarn over and pull up a loop. Yarn over and draw through 2 loops. Yarn over and draw through two loops again. Yarn over twice, insert hook in same stitch, yarn over and pull up a loop, yarn over and draw through two loops, yarn over and draw through 2 loops (you should now have 3 loops on hook.) **

For a **tr2tog**, yarn over and draw through the last 3 loops on the hook to complete the tr2tog.

For a **tr3tog,** do * to ** as described above, but to create the third trtog, you will need to yarn over twice, insert the hook into designated stitch again and then yarn over and draw up a loop, yarn over and draw through 2 loops, yarn over and draw through 2 more loops, (you'll have 4 loops on the hook), yarn over and draw through all 4 loops on the hook. You have now created a **tr3tog cluster/bobble.**

About the Artist & Designer

Kristen Stein is an award-winning Contemporary Artist living in Suburban Philadelphia. Kristen's works are currently available on a variety of online venues and boutiques and galleries throughout the US. Her art has appeared in numerous printed media including posters, books, CD Covers, calendars and program covers. Her work has been licensed for use on gift items, household goods, puzzles and jewelry items. Her work has appeared in a number of solo and group exhibitions and in the set design for various television shows and a major motion picture. Although the bulk of her portfolio focuses on her original paintings and designs, Kristen also enjoys needlework and creating her own original crochet patterns. A self-proclaimed "espresso aficionado", Kristen is still trying to master the latte art technique. Although, nowhere near perfecting the technique, she still enjoys every delicious attempt.

Please visit http://kristensteinfineart.blogspot.com or http://StudioArtworks.com for more information.

On Instagram & TikTok: @kristensteindesigns.

Made in the USA
Columbia, SC
15 August 2023